Heavy and Light

by Rod Theodorou and Carole Telford

Contents

RIGBY
INTERACTIVE LIBRARY

© 1996 Rigby Education
Published by Rigby Interactive Library,
an imprint of Rigby Education,
division of Reed Elsevier, Inc.
500 Coventry Lane
Crystal Lake, IL 60014

Illustrations by Gwen Tourret and Trevor Dunton
Color reproduction by Track QSP
Printed in China

00 99 98 97 96
10 9 8 7 6 5 4 3 2 1

ISBN 1-57572-061-2

Library Cataloging-in-Publication Data

Library of Congress Cataloging-in-Publication Data
Theodorou, Rod.
    Heavy and light / by Rod Theodorou and Carole Telford;
[illustrations by Sheila Townsend and Trevor Dunton].
        p.   cm. — (Animal opposites)
    Includes index.
    Summary: Compares the habitat, feeding patterns, and behavior of the
hippopotamus and hummingbird as determined by their physical attributes.
    ISBN 1-57572-061-2 (lib. bdg.)
    1. Animals—Juvenile literature. 2. Hippopotamus—Juvenile literature.
3. Hummingbirds—Juvenile literature. 4. Body weight—Juvenile literature.
[1. Hippopotamus. 2. Hummingbirds.] I. Telford, Carole, 1961–
II. Townsend, Sheila, ill. III. Dunton, Trevor, ill. IV. Title.
V. Series: Theodorou, Rod. Animal opposites.
QL49.T3475   1996
591.5—dc20   95-36314
                                                                         CIP
                                                                          AC

Photographic Acknowledgments
Andrew Plumptre/OSF p4; Stan Osolinski/OSF p5; Carol Farneti/Partridge Films Ltd/OSF p6;
Michael Fogden/OSF p7; Bruce Davidson p8, back cover; Robert A Tyrrell/OSF pp9, 13, 15, 17, 21;
Root/Okapia/OSF p10; Marie Read/Bruce Coleman Ltd p11; Richard Packwood/OSF pp12, 14, 20; Daniel J
Cox/OSF p16; Tom Leach/OSF p18; Jen and Des Bartlett/Bruce Coleman Ltd p19
Front cover: Mark Petersen/Tony Stone Images; Robert A Tyrrell/OSF

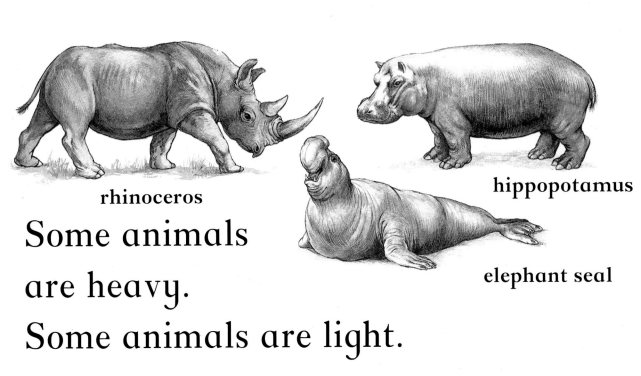

rhinoceros

hippopotamus

elephant seal

Some animals
are heavy.
Some animals are light.

butterfly

bat

hummingbird

This is a hippopotamus.
Hippos are big and heavy.

This is a hummingbird.
Hummingbirds are
small and light.

5

Hippos live in Africa.
They like to live by a river.

Most hummingbirds live in
hot places.
Many live in North and
South America.

Big hippos are very heavy.
They weigh as much as 50 people!
Even lions do not attack them.

Hummingbirds are
smaller than any other bird.
Some are as light as butterflies.

Hippos move slowly on land.
Under water, they can move fast.

Hummingbirds fly very fast.
Their wings flap so quickly,
they make a humming sound.

Hippos have special big teeth to scare off enemies.
They have other strong teeth to chew plants.

Hummingbirds have long bills and very long tongues. This helps them reach inside flowers to eat.

bill

tongue

13

Hippos spend most of the
day in the water.
The water keeps them cool.

Hummingbirds are always on
the move.
They spend most of the day eating.

Hippos need to eat lots of plants. They come out of the water every night to eat.

Hummingbirds eat insects and spiders. They suck sweet nectar from inside flowers.

Mother hippos have one baby a year.
Even baby hippos love the mud!

Hummingbird nests are about
the size of a quarter.
A mother hummingbird lays one or
two tiny eggs each year.

Sometimes baby hippos climb on an adult to keep safe from crocodiles.

5-day old chicks

The mother
hummingbird
looks after
her tiny
chicks.
She brings
them insects
to eat.

AMAZING FACTS!

Hippo tusks are as long as your arm!

Hippos can hold their breath for 5 minutes.

Hummingbirds are the only birds that can fly backwards!

Some hummingbirds steal flies from spiders' webs!

GRRR!

"﬚"

Index